Kitty Donnelly

The Impact of Limited Time

Indigo Dreams Publishing

First Edition: The Impact of Limited Time
First published in Great Britain in 2020 by:
Indigo Dreams Publishing
24, Forest Houses
Cookworthy Moor
Halwill
Beaworthy
Devon
EX21 5UU

www.indigodreams.co.uk

Kitty Donnelly has asserted her/his right under the Copyright, Designs and Patents Act 1988 to be identified as the author of this work.

ISBN 978-1-912876-40-2

British Library Cataloguing in Publication Data. A CIP record for this book can be obtained from the British Library.

Designed and typeset in Palatino Linotype by Indigo Dreams.
Cover design by Ronnie Goodyer at Indigo from original
'Illustrazione Lizzie Siddal, la musa dei preraffaelliti,
Daniela Matarazzo 2015'
Printed and bound in Great Britain by 4edge Ltd.
Papers used by Indigo Dreams are recyclable products made from wood grown in sustainable forests following the guidance of the Forest Stewardship Council.

For Hugo Donnelly 1951-2003,
who taught me to value limited time,
for Evie & for M.

Acknowledgements

'Stella Sculps the Murderer' is based on the character Stella Raphael, from Patrick McGrath's novel *Asylum*.

Acknowledgements are due to the editors of the following: *Acumen, The American Journal of Poetry, Big Lit, The Beautiful Space, Creative Future Anthology, The Dawntreader, The Fenland Reed, Message in a Bottle, Mslexia, The New Welsh Review, Nine Muses Poetry, Quadrant, Sentinel Literary Quarterly, Wild Atlantic Words.*

In 2016, 'Migration' was commended in the *Southport Writers' Circle Competition*. 'Night At Whitestone Farm' was long-listed for the *Canterbury University Poet of the Year*, 2016. 'Lizzie Siddal' and 'Pudding Lane' were long-listed for *The Plough Prize* in 2018. In 2019, 'Limited Time' was shortlisted for the *York Mix Poetry Competition*; 'The 'flat tops'' won a *Creative Future* award. 'Greenwich Foot Tunnel' was commended in the *McLellan Poetry Prize*.

I couldn't wish for more supportive publishers than Dawn and Ronnie at Indigo Dreams. Thanks also to the tutors and students on the MA Creative Writing Programme at Manchester Metropolitan University, Class of 2019/20 for all your feedback, inspiration and constructive criticism. I would not have had the confidence to publish this book without Malcolm Benson's editorial input, wine and humour (all hours of day and night). Susan Donnelly has given me her time and her sharp, critical eye and supported me all the way. 'Fall' is for Sarah Donnelly, who has lived many of these poems. I am grateful to Kath Burlinson for decades of positivity and encouragement.

i.m of Bridget English, who truly knew what kindness is.

CONTENTS

The Impact of Limited Time

Time

So we plough each week
into a furrow of the past.

Do you feel that dull insistence?
That's time

tugging at your substance
like a thread

spooling from the wheel
then spent.

Between the Worlds

The sky looked as it's never looked again.
On the tips of our tongues, revelations.

All day the giddy colours of a dream,
then the lucidity of darkness.

A sunset infused with such terminal red
it shocked the whole harbor at Fishbourne.

Heightened senses, discarded reticence –
these were our compensations.

Birds in the Hospital

Dawn barely hatched, birds knew the berries
were utterly ready. *Turn onto your left side, please –*
They'd been pecking the stitches of darkness
like eager children plucking at birthday wrappings.
Now the narrow slot between ripe and rot was open,
they arrived in a plume: every branch abush – *hurts*
if I press here? Or here? – yes, *abush,* the right description –
freckled bibs of song thrush, robins resting for a whistle
between beakfulls – *lie still, use your gas and air –*
fieldfare, redwing, relaying down the wind's funnels.
Once they'd stripped the holly – *sharp scratch –*
back to waxy, winter plumage, a blackbird
translated the day into verse from the theatre's roof
and the act was done. *I'm removing the scope now, deep breath –*

A Year in the Butcher's Flat

Every night they came that spring:
refrigerated trucks throbbing like hearts
and the butcher's brother,
sprawled in the doorway in blankets.
By day, we found green bottles
discarded and hollow pigs,
hooked behind the sign *Good Meat*.
Chernobyl's fallout drifted, a toxic
scarf on the wind, and the butcher
scrawled *Our Lamb Not Welsh*
on a hunk of cardboard.
I was either thrilled or frightened
that long summer Suzie Lamplugh
                              vanished,
leaping to the *Fame* theme in a leotard
like the last blind fling of childhood.
As leaves timed their release,
we saw dad less and less.
I ate his oven-shrivelled dinners.
When winter stole into classrooms,
seeping from wellies and macs,
I made Suzie my end-of-term project,
screening my face with *Matilda*
when my eyes filled –
till Ms Hood shrilled:
Are you bawling for that estate agent?
She's probably run away to get married.

Off Comers

First the kids lined up outside.
Their silent vigil lasted
and their parents' eyes
tracked us like searchlights
through the boredom of their summer
when subtlety cracks like a river bed.

Our garden became
an ashtray, a dogs' toilet.
We woke to eggshells
splayed across the path,
OFF COMERS
sprayed in fat red lettering.

On the bus, a girl gobbed
in my pigtails,
held a lighter to my coat.
It raged that autumn –
rising with the school-term:
a conflagration of hatred.

Rubble

I came to run, a final time, the halls
where Mr H dropped pens to squat
and peer under our obligatory skirts;

to recall us in prefab classrooms
whispering truths, and sprouting
from the rubble of our childhoods.

I came too late, the school's already dust.
Weeds have leapt to waist-height, undisturbed.
Gulls sense disquiet, roosting on once-goalposts.

I remember an Ecstasy pill rolling out
of a geography book; your pottery doll,
her eyes lolled back like a girl in overdose;

the man who yelled your name
through the woodchip wall as he came
in your mam, how she resented you for it.

I was a vessel of your secrets
almost twenty-seven years,
until our friendship clicked, a spent cassette, to silence.

I came to conjure us.
Racing from the science block to maths,
you link my arm, and all our hope's in touching distance.

There's a storm far out on the Solway Firth.

Caesarean

From the off I should have claimed you,
clutched you to my skin,
cradled you as Mary would've done.

When my womb was slit behind a sheet,
dividing sight from insides opened,
teeth clacking with a cartoon, epidural cold

and sickness lapping like the seventh wave
at high tide, they placed you in my arms.
Students, beckoned over, gawped

into my specimen, practising illegible scrawls.
The anaesthetist gave a thumbs-down to a doctor
across the steely, blue-lit stage of theatre.

I passed you to another – unable to hold
both my own blind fear and the expectation
brightening eyes already flickering to focus.

Threat

After 39 weeks of harbouring you
in the core of myself,
we were public property, you and I –
bodies pried, behaviour scrutinised.

It was all about roles so suddenly.
To hold you and translate the world was not enough.
I watched for changes in your face,
currents in your mood, pains passing like clouds.

Distant family dangled you:
your neck lolling over the lips of their elbows.
They kissed you on the mouth,
testing your milk on their tongues.

I saw spirals of bacteria, spikes of virus.
Cringing away to the bedroom,
I shielded my ears from a flat of intruders,
sneezing and clearing their throats.

The Still Woman

She climbed down the rungs of herself
to reach this space – forgetting
how her frayed tongue lapped at the well of wishes,
what those wishes could have been.
What shocked them most is that she offered
no excuses – allowing nothing,
as though nothing was hers for the taking.
They expected explanations.
They expected her to *want*.

A tree's being felled by the railway line.
She's on her side, her knees drawn up,
this static woman. Hearing chainsaws
grunting through the bark, she senses
woods' resistance – *give* – shift into stillness.

Cave Painting

Pass me the horse hair brush steeped in colours of earth.
I will paint you our beginnings.

In sleep, you flee from leopards, bison, wolves.
Harness their dream-spirits,

tame them on the walls, and you'll rest fearless.
Your loss is charcoal-black;

your anger – a quiver of hematite arrows;
the calcite-white of your silence/a curtain between us.

Daughter, we can't linger in this cave-light.
Time's a virus plundering our settlements.

We must immortalise our hands
in ochre, umber, malachite.

Border Town

Fistfuls of nights you watch them burn –
Sean, Aidan, Seamus.
You try but cannot break the glass

of dream to save them, wake
imprinted by their fingers
grasping for purchase.

Then another lad from class: his grin
a premature flash of teeth
as his greeting's torn from his tongue.

This, a Tuesday. A British town.
You fled – I was born
to peace, a leafy street.

What you couldn't comprehend,
the tap tap tap
of the typewriter told.

I sat on the bottom step and listened,
the comfort of your jumper turning cold
when you spoke a name aloud –

every syllable sharp –
the way you'd enunciate
names of the murdered.

The 'flat tops'

they called this chain of concrete prefabs.
Two years here, the rent man said,
n'they upgrade you to one
at t'other end. With a roof.

A desiccated mouse
hid in the workings
of our hand-out cooker.
Life went backwards.

I slept in my school uniform that autumn,
dreading the dawn chorus.
My tongue
turned against me.

By the coal hole at night
I watched chimneys breathe in unison.
Our own fire
laboured to smoulder.

In the crescent where graffiti swore
fuck this fuck that
I dialled Childline
'cos it was free: the listener

a touch too keen for each instalment.
It was my own voice I chased
down the wire and found,
unjudged but flat as parchment.

Church of Sweets

After the Hundreds and Thousands,
we consider eating toothpaste.
We've had almost enough of each other:
my skin beneath your nails, your hair in my fist.
Instead, we raid the sofa's grit for pennies.

Where a fat TV spills wiry guts, and the old Jack Russell
leaps like an orange spring to the brim of the fence,
we train our vision on the newsagent's beacon,
swearing on sweets
to be good all week if only it's open.

We tongue blackberry chews: the ultimate
machine-made fruit; whorled pink
shells of candy shrimp; flying saucers;
Penicillin-smelling foam bananas.
A prism of flavours explode

in sugar communion
then and there on split linoleum.
Darkness leers through the glass, its features familiar.
The shopkeeper smiles at the gratitude
tumbling from our Brilliant Blue tongues.

Crawl

The hallway warns: *No Prams No Pushchairs.*
Your practiced fingers navigate the dark –
deadening the rustle of the rain shield,
fastening taut belt straps with one hand
for the pre-dawn winter crawl up Corn Street.

When shops are shielded by shutters
and a full moon loiters purposefully over the park;
in the hour when poetry reels
through your veins and arteries,
when phrases pester a heart
three-quarters gifted to a daughter,
you lug a nappy bag of broken verse and climb,
impulses kicking in the harnesses of parenthood,
mother-tongue now nursery rhyme.

Relapse

Too long I wondered why he cast off belts
in every room, shed skins;

how tinfoil crept into unusual places,
scorched and folded into hidden spaces.

Sunken-eyed, before hard evidence, still he lied.
I smashed every matching, aubergine dish.

Twelve weeks after those bold blue lines lit up the strip,
I lay with jelly smeared across my stomach,

a sonographer probing the screen. Her face read
something's wrong while he scored in East Oxford.

His key stopped turning in the lock.
The dawn became my own.

Comforted by the kicks and tumbles,
as sun crawled through the bars of the estate,

I thought him dead so many times
he was – until he wasn't.

Whitestone Farm

The moon is almost fully waxed –
the ghost of the inevitable
already visible.

Now on the frost-cast hillside
something catches the eye,
warming the lens:

a fire lit in the valley's pit, lit
and burning steadily.
Although too far to taste its heat,

it's the volt of hope
in the human heart
when those first sparks leapt from the flint.

Crossing Over

I remember our voices
mixing in the evenings;
destinationless drives
on Good Fridays, while all
Chichester queued for the retail park.

Now as a red kite soars above Eskdale
and the *S* of a song thrush
skips between lambs,
forgetting its wings –
now as the rock diverts the river –

I remember my arm
through the crook of your arm
as you lean, prematurely.
Taking your weight, we cross Westgate,
entering a house, still brightly lit.

Limited Time

So the lady opposite mentions
that my cat sprints back and forth
across the Burnley Road.

I ask in desperation:
does he look, though? Even a glance?
No, I'm told. He bolts despite wheels.

When the cat-flap snaps
and he waits for his meat,
I see him differently.

Now he wonders:
Why the tuna? Extra lap-time? –
rolling his territory's grit on the duvet.

Life's short, I tell him, running
my hand through his winter coat.
Perhaps he's had a similar notion

creeping through the bulbless cellar,
climbing stairs, checking the bed – unslept in –
feeling: *the good times are over.*

I Used to Work Here Once

A husk of darkness swallows
those last seeds of light
fighting the horizon
where Knaresborough castle stands
tall as a knight, resilient.
Birds sing each other home,
calves are quiet. A girl scales
stile and furrow, the cycle of seasons
ingrained in her bones, as tide
ridges rock, or rings of an oak
map winters without nourishment.
No stir or bark, she crosses the yard –
departing where a door once stood.

Mr Sparks

Something was wrong with Mr Sparks
the day he came calling.

Street-lights sprang into early action.
There was a storm-feeling.

All afternoon, he lingered in our living room,
repeating words and phrases,

stroking his own arm.
When the power cut, mum sent him home.

He went not home
but all the way to Belarus, land of a lost girlfriend.

When he returned, his features had softened.
Bland and satisfied, hunger had gone.

He lumbered, grinning brokenly.
Psychosis, mum whispered.

I rolled the word across my tongue,
tasting its potency.

Woodman

You fetch cleaved oak for the fire,
telling how the branch died –

dead heart a hollow stem
revealed in cutting.

Then a birch log felled alive,
heavier, its core still running

brightly through the centre.
Whether lightening-struck,

starved from the root,
or a bark-stripped skeleton

elm in lowland, you see only
their usefulness, seasoned,

making of my superstitions
fuel to survive the cold.

Field Mouse in the Rat Trap

A volt of loose lightening,
it bolted the cage –

the bead of its eye a frenzy
nothing but freedom could tranquilise.

I was afraid its little tempest would implode
before the safety of the hedge.

In a week when ceilings fell in,
it was a wild thing,

immune to our sufferings, sourced
from a deep, old world.

Swansea on the Rocks

I thought it was named Wind Street, as in blow, gust, gale.
In the bar they laughed good-naturedly.
It's wind love, as in twist, curve, coil.

In the BHS café, macs were slung on chair backs.
Old ladies smoked and coughed over their chips.
My leased walls spored a mouldy, weeping damp.

I didn't cut my arms, or take the pills
I'd collected as insurance.
I listened to Eva Cassidy instead,

dying bleached hair back to its dark roots.
My manager, preferring blondes,
called me Ozzy after that –

still groping my arse as I brought him his coffee.
In my diary I wrote of Cerys, a fellow PA,
who had Wednesday as Special Leave:

I need abnormal cells burnt off my cervix.
It's better than work. I'm dead sick of this office.
And they give you a biscuit, after, like. With tea.

A noose of cloud enclosed the bay that evening
as I washed my hands in brine,
wondering how I'd beached up here –

if pain recedes like the ocean's silty tongue.

Age of 37

The Spring you left, I aged ten years.
My eyes sagged, tired of seeing.

All thirty-seven summers of pleasing
were suddenly scribed onto skin.

My hair lost lustre, accepting grey,
relinquishing false colour.

You left the way illusions fracture,
or a poem – fully formed in sleep –

evaporates on touching
the litmus test of dawn.

Giving Evidence

I'll remember the cheap clock always,
ticking off the letters of the law,

a leaf-shaped stain on the empty chair,
the probe of the sergeant's voice.

I hid my face like a child or a dog,
ears listening regardless.

Then the tape's click: your hand
shivering above the statement.

It had rained when we came out –
the Derwent black and nearing flood-mark.

You said, *he'll be free till he dies, the bastard.*
I turned my eyes to the wind,

needing the bad man's heart
to be weighed against the feather,

for somewhere to be safe, or sacred.

After the Solstice

The longest day swings on its hinge.
Newspapers smoulder with division.

This lick of political flames won't be drowned
by a flash summer flood so fierce

our enemy rabbits hutch together, fur on fur.
We listen to the downpour, caught

between flash and thunder in our
half-finished, half-purchased house.

What future lies in ambush
for your sons, my daughter?

Envelopes

Let them spore on the doormat:
    council demands
        red-topped statements
            court summons.

Let bailiffs bang their meaty fists
and dust dull the unmoving curtains.

Let the meter turn
    through the switch stuck on,
        let rates increase
            though taps never run.

She can't be fined, filmed, ticketed, threatened.
However far their systems reach

they cannot touch her now
    and there's No
        Forwarding
            Address.

Pudding Lane

The Great Fire of London started on Pudding Lane on 2nd September 1666 in the bakery of Thomas Farriner. The first victim was believed to be his maidservant who refused to climb out of a top floor window with the family.

They blamed my master Thomas and his oven.
It was I, I with a candle,
unable to settle, pacing the floor.

Grandmother never slept.
She spent her drawn-out life awaiting rest,
staring from stale mattresses.

Mother died, an escapologist.
This was my inheritance.
All summer I burned

in servants' quarters,
unable to stand the stench of the Thames.
A headache gnawed,

a fevered claustrophobia.
Tenements inched closer,
timbers touching noses over alleyways,

fetid air   combustible,
and each inhabitant
a match, ready to flare.

She takes the room in Miller's Court

despite the murder,
insisting John McCarthy mend both glass and lock,
dries stockings over a rickety chair, paces
the square worn under *The Fisherman's Widow*,
in step with her predecessor.
Every doss house, every tenement
knows violence, she consoles herself,
ignoring tell-tale stains behind the wash-stand.
She's bold till firelight weakens,
when shadows sway and leap like puppet's hands.

Her thoughts circle back to the dead woman,
also charged five shillings
for four mouldy walls, no bolt,
who heard the Christ Church bells cry out in loneliness,
a mug of gin in reach
to drown the strangers' smells and slurs.
Now the tenant wakes to a lilting voice:
two words she strains to hear,
sure it's a name, unclear: a secret
told by a sister, sleep-talking though a door, ajar.

The Day the Leaves Let Go

We were up till 3am, not knowing
the Day the Leaves Let Go had begun.
Out there in the dark they were already falling.

When we woke, still lousy with sleep
and the tang of rum on our tongues,
they were in full flow.

The day of the Wedding of Seasons
when air turned the bend from another mild autumn,
confetti rained, celebrating the bite of Calder wind,

its teeth already locked-on.
You shook a bough and every leaf
was swinging and releasing.

The bathroom floor was christened with them,
                                sneaking in
where shower-steam streamed out into the cold.

The Tuna-thing

He lived on sandwiches.
Kept nothing in his fridge
but milk and Daddies Sauce.

Testing the cupboard's strangeness
with our fingers, we found prunes,
Angel Delight, satsumas in syrup.

When we weren't at Little Chef,
or poking fish and chips
with wooden forks, he'd say

Right girls! Tonight
I'll make the tuna-thing,
rolling up his shirt-sleeves,

chopping onions with precision
straight onto the worktop
of whatever rented place he was in.

While he cooked, we'd type –
then Tipex out – rude words,
or seek evidence of his new existence:

a Lincoln Imp on the fireplace,
an Abbeville street map,
a note signed *Rod.*

Stella Sculpts the Murderer

When I get bored watching my marriage
wither on the vine, I conjure your image.

I sculpt you without fantasy,
without moulding away your savagery.

Sometimes I run my tongue along
your coarse, clay cheeks.

I have lost touch with my own face.
The mirror takes and won't return.

Last night, lying apart from you,
I dreamed I was Cassiopeia –

Ethiopian queen of constellations.
I ruled my kingdoms

with dirty hands and an ill-fitting gown.
When I woke, the light discharged

a warmth, like blood.
Then you were there, *persisting*.

Lizzie Siddal

He sketched me once in Highgate
when waning light betrayed his charcoal,
failed his eyesight.

He cursed he couldn't
catch my profile as it was.
I was patient and I ached.

As laudanum enters the bloodstream,
the mind numbs and elucidates.
Tonight my hair won't be put out –

a fire before the glass.
In oils they never captured it so luminous.
At first I thought them moths, lured to its flame.

It was I who singed my wings,
I who crave these bitter tears
the vial spills on my tongue.

Cracks

Perhaps you should accept
the sadness in your heart

as those who choose the coast
must suffer squalls of wind.

Your skin is paper-thin.
You are painful to look at.

Every fish has stilled
with this high tide.

Tears flow easy as a spring,
loosed from the aquifer.

Your bruises have re-blemished.
You taste earth.

Animals in the Same Cage

We twitch like rabbits
caught in the rungs of nightmare,
your damp hand heavy on my thigh
where scars glow
lunar-white in childhood's glare.

Often you leap to your feet,
eager in sleep to fight
the one who soldered bars,
who blocked those natural runs
you would have followed,

as I wake again to the click of the lock
and absence, hardening shadows.

**Relative Who Leapt From His Breakfast
and Was Never Seen Again**

Was it the monotony of morning, its blasé light
drowsing in the room where the Virgin
promised, over the mantel, *all's eternally well*?

Was it the sooty hollows thumbed
beneath his Noreen's eyes, the way sausages stacked
against quartered toast, how oil from a fried egg

slicked towards the beans?
I must get the paper! He leapt: his abruptness
disrupting particles of dust. The terrier stood, then sat.

No one saw him turn onto the street.
We were told that his black overcoat retained
his shape on the rack, for months.

The breakfast became a *tableau*.
Loyally by the door, the wiry terrier waited
in character, mourning for a master

that not only did not come, but never came.
            I know what it is to find yourself
on the edge of yourself

when you thought there was running to do,
when you rolled your dice with a fighting chance
but all your hope was burning out of view

behind the curtain of your coping. Is this where he was
that coatless February, with pockets of cold questions
jangling like coins long out of currency?

Sundowning

In 2019 they sing *Pack Up Your Troubles.*
Behind a mural of blue skies,
locked doors. *Where am I Mavis?* –
Replies are butterflies – touching the mind,
alighting. Ask again.
You're in Birch Bank. Yes, Harry's coming.
Wanderings through a painted land.
False bookshelves, Jubilee flags all year 'round.

After sundown she looks beyond you
as though through broken glass, remembering
only her incantations. At her chant,
the unit bristles till each resident finds voice
and nurses rush to tranquillise the sound
before it perforates the boundaries of the heard world.

Dusk in an Empty House

A bird's alarm call
warns from the hawthorn,
startling a heart now torn

from the canal dream,
        the phone box dream,
                the dream that really happened.

I wake to the pulse of the fridge,
wind in wires,
tears no threads can stitch.

Here's only I,
and I
to manage.

Counteraction

Circuit Bar   a colleague torching forwards
you're a delight to catch in here   instinct cast-off
laughter rediscovered language   first night in months
other than mother   freedom   almost
taxi   *walk ahead in case the neighbours see*
why   why   stumbling   *quickly quickly*
warnings blinking furiously   too late
disarray   beaded curtains shoved aside
heart-shaped frames pink as Puma schoolbags
Jenny & Friends   wrongness in the spirit's pit
a last blast of capacity   *don't look at those get over here*
                heft of a body –

cold miles   head down   sick   sicker
razor blade pains   willing the windscreen
thaw quicker   numb   number than winter –
later   *i'll jump off a bridge*   *if you tell her I'm done*
balled in the bathroom   Crayola bruises
mixing in the palette of the dermis
          pressed hard enough   a page tears
my daughter's calling needing me downstairs
I weigh my mucky heart   against the feather
of her voice   & go   we watch *Horrible Histories*
jaws working Haribo   in unison
as though this were the equal and the opposite reaction –

Fall

before towers had fallen
before cells misfired and multiplied
before we had the language to describe
what we were sheltered from
when we loved and were loved
where shadows were long

there were pale summer afternoons
when midges hovered low in clouds
and apples from the garden
shrank our tongues with sourness
where we ran ragged   leaping streams
unselfconscious as animals

for you I would gather the fragments of his voice
I would sweep them and piece them
like shredded notes
I would score the sounds of the wind
for the tunes of his speech
and record each one if it took decades

It's not routinely so painful to watch, said the nurse,
the transition's usually ... without such a fight –

outside the window all our childhood afternoons
in one final blaze were fading and the light
was sad and beautiful   streaming in
on something broken and unfixable
like a sun from a far climate that has known
completeness   the joy of a self whole

Aftermath

All afternoon blonde spools of heat
unraveled on the lawn

till late light mourned
a fire extinguished,

a stunned house gasped
and the room was closed.

I'd expected relief –
emptying draws of pharmaceuticals,

bagging clothes, I'd expected
to take a breath,

but all the wilted air was used
and leaves were turning.

One death's not death done,
nor the future intact, but a slow reassembling.

We'll meet again perhaps
on the other side of suffering.

Crime Scene

After the act, they scissor
my scarlet sleeve to the elbow,

rooting for a vein: bare arm
a just-hatched wound, tepid

with bruises, magnetising shadow.
I'm turned. My back displays

a constellation of door handles –
cupboard corners lining-up

like fresh formations of stars.
I watch from rising distance

my own crime scene stumbled on
too late: my mother's morals,

my father's mind
diluted, leaking onto concrete.

Answerphone

There's nothing here but pain
and your phone ringing
     and ringing
where nobody answers,
and answers constantly with silence.

Greenwich Foot Tunnel

For his coffin
he chose the irises
his mother brought him
in a dream.
I'm thinking of him
now as I descend
at Cutty Sark
to river-cold,
water-weight.
I'm thinking
this is how it
might've been –
dying, being torn
from the day
to walk beneath
dripping cast-
iron – leaving
food-stalls, faces,
reams and reams
of photographs.
Attempting to shout:
Stop! I need those!
(*need those*, echoing),
knowing a word
is happening
that won't find
the tip of your tongue –
light spreading
like untrodden snow –
relief. Then letting go.

Migration

All night I listen to the fair being dismantled,
lie imagining the carousel disbanded, horse by horse;

the unbagging of goldfish; that longed-for rush
as lost coins fill the mouths of Penny Falls.

The sycamore's shawlless.
Frost sprinkles tiny gemstones on our flower beds.

Goose-pimpled legs chase covers.
Suddenly hedgerows are restless

with seeds of flight, sewn in a dream.
Now as light, sliced by the blind,

steepens its gradient, ticking engines
wait to migrate to the cold roads of England.

On ponds and wetlands,
geese arrive in formations.

Indigo Dreams Publishing Ltd
24, Forest Houses
Cookworthy Moor
Halwill
Beaworthy
Devon
EX21 5UU
www.indigodreams.co.uk